Title:

Pathway to

Self-Healing

A Journey to Self-Love and Happiness

Copyright

Copyright 2021 by:

Eva Ghale Mistry

Preface

The SELF and Healing are two conjectures that many today are hopelessly stuck to the attempts at their interlinking. Whenever we get hurt as humans, the aftermath usual is a picture of us battered and seeming helpless. For many, a soul, body and mind like that is apparently incapable of healing the SELF. "Remedy must come from the outside" would be the verdict. This piece, however, projects a deviation from the conventional. Leveling the trio of science, experience, and multilayered intellect and insights, the Author shows the possibility of healing, repositioning and emancipation all happening from the within of the SELF as well as reeling out the physical, spiritual and psychological preconditions for that to take place. Capturing the Theta state of the mind, Angels Energy, and Buddhism amongst others as the accessory techniques to utilise for the objective to be achieved, this book concludes that although there are many conceptual pathways to self-healing, they are only functional at the will and instance of one entity – YOU.

Acknowledgments

The many clients and students I've worked with and taught over the years and have shared their wellness journeys and inspired me with their courage and determination to heal.

My family and friends for always being there. You know who you are and what you mean to me; the world.

I can't thank you enough for everything, my caring husband Dipan, and my two lovely children Eugene and Elithea. You are my life, and I love you dearly.

My mother Mina, I am so grateful for all of the love and support through my life-long wellness journey. Without having you in my corner, I don't know where I would be today!

To all those ready to embrace their healing journey, may these pages serve as a good resource for your journey. May they inspire you to make choices that best suit your wellness needs.

I am eternally grateful to all who have helped me on this amazing in life. It is an honor to contribute or share with you what I've learned or experienced throughout this journey here within these pages. It is also humbling for me to do so.

Table of Contents

Dedication

This book is dedicated to my brother Bishesh Ghale who died seven years ago. Bishesh was an amazing person whom I would have loved to see again. He was a compassionate, caring, loving, and beautiful soul. We looked alike but were very different in many ways.

We shared the same womb for nine months, and it took us another eighteen years to grow together as adults. I will never forget our talks, his smile, the way he smelled, the clothes he wore. Just thinking about him makes my heart ache with sadness and happiness at the same time. If I could have one day with him or just a few minutes to talk about life, love, family, dreams, and the universe again, I would relish it.

I wish I had more time to get to know Bishesh because he did not show me the full extent of his personality. Bishesh journeyed through many dark valleys in his life, which is part of what made him crave to drink. He was a caring and loving individual who sought love in all the wrong places, so it would not be found when he needed it most.

I'm very grateful for my time with Bishesh, even though we did not spend much quality time together when we were adults. It was painful when you left. I wish we could experience my daughter together, even if it were for a few glimpses.

I love you, Bishesh.

You made this journey with me in spirit, even though you were not around in the body. You showed me that I could face fear head-on, never say die, and do my best to be a good person. You encouraged me to follow my heart so I could be happy even though you couldn't do it yourself.

I hope you are still following your dreams, wherever you are. If there is anything more I could have done for you, please forgive me because I am grateful for our short time together. I pray you are alive and well in the world of spirit.

Love, Eva

About the Author

Eva is a healer, teacher, writer, and wife. She was born in Nepal, where things were rough and challenging for her as a little girl. Becoming a Theta healing Instructor was something more than a coincidence for her. It indeed feels like she was destined to be an apostle of this technique, using it to better the lives of people around the world and provide training to others interested in knowing the psychosocial and spiritual relevance of Theta healing to mental and physical challenges.

After taking and excelling in extensive training courses at various levels, she became an Angel healing teacher certified to provide qualitative learning developments in the subject. She has also travelled across the world to improve her skill.

So it went like this, In 2006, which was a very challenging year for Eva, she visited the Shirdi Sai Baba Temple in India after going through major emotional traumas, and she was healed from her pains and sorrow. She was not new to spiritual healing, but as heaven wants it, the visit to the temple had a great impact on her journey.

So many of her childhood traumas are healed, and the memories which were repressed become awake. After experiencing the wholesomeness and the healing she got in the meditation exercises, she committed to taking more and more people on the healing journey.

Ever since Eva has been helping people from all walks of life, those who have been struggling with psychosocial and spiritual aspects heal from different pains and struggles. Today, she is an International ThetaHealing Instructor and an Angel teacher herself. If you want to contact Eva directly, please use the following email Instagram: @evaghalemistry, Facebook: @evaghalemistry YouTube: @evaghalemistry Website: **www.evaghalemistry.com**. Eva lives with her loving husband and her two kids in the UK.

Letter to Readers

The world is full of pain. We can feel it in each other's eyes, hear it in each other's voices, and sense it when we shake hands or embrace one another after an absence. Pain has many faces and countless expressions but whatever its forms, pain is universal. It knows no boundaries of time, culture, religion, gender, social status, special interests, and age group. I have passed through pain also, and I understand what you are passing through. I can feel your pain because I was once like you.

There is no situation so bad with life's challenges that we cannot overcome it or at least alleviate some of the discomforts if not cure ourselves completely. The choice is ours, whether we will utilise the resources available to us or sit idly by waiting for someone else to help us!

There are no shortcuts to wellness. The pain must be faced and worked through. Nobody can replace you to make that effort, but once we take over our healing process, it is a message of hope, a decentralised system, self-regulating and self-directing.

Your journey towards wellness begins with your first step forward. Look at this as an opportunity for growth and change rather than as an insurmountable obstacle or as punishment for something wrong you did. You can do it! I believe in you!

Sincerely yours,
Eva Ghale

Chapter One

Introduction - YOU and the World

Why is the world against me? This is a question you have asked yourself numerous times. But have you ever found an answer? Now, ask yourself a simple question; Who am I? Pause a second and answer yourself. Now is the time for you to cut down that tree you are sitting on, spread your wings, and fly like a bird because something about you is about to be discovered.

YOU are not just the physical you. Your existence as a human being is featured in three dimensions of life – the body, mind, and soul. The three systems that make up every human work together to form a whole. Simply put, you are because of the possibilities of these three dimensions of yourself. The body marks our physical presence in this world and is receptive and hosts the two other aspects. Things of the world do take their tolls on us in one or more of the three ways. We do get hurt and have pains in our bodies. This is the same way our minds can get badly bruised by things that happen to us. Our souls can be in real agony for these bad experiences, and we are left with adverse effects on the other aspects of the self.

Being part of this world means we are not immune to the pains and hardships that come with it. Still, it is believed that everyone has been equipped with the inner infrastructure to pursue happiness and fulfillment. We only need personal determination, guidance, and the right approaches to bring out these potentials and achieve success with them.

Our potentials are always available, but our duty as individuals is to make the best out of it. Life itself has shown us perspectives that do not conform to realities about ourselves. Some are even based on denial or repression of the self. The denial may be blatant or outright. We choose not to pay attention to it because we do not want to believe what we don't feel, see or hear. Even if we do, we would stubbornly believe that it is a hallucination.

The other perspective of life is repression – This is how we repress ourselves and gag our feelings, emotions, and beliefs - defining the discipline. We chose to live in a circle, and it kept coming back at us. Discipline is the key to losing the chain that captures us.

What could best fit discipline? Rather than giving expressions to these cravings and finding how to realise or manage them in such a way that the purpose of life is not defeated, we rather go on to defy these. Rather, we tend to put out and live a life that fits that picture endorsed by the weak part of us. It becomes easy for us to do this because society has taught us how to live and the dreams we should live for. On society's table, these options are limited, so not fitting in may mean losing out.

Right from conception, the world already has its expectations marked out. Usually, these standards are the result of the world's opinions about life itself. But it is only logical that, since life is personal to the person alive, living should also be – why should it correspond to some opinions and traditions that may not have anything to do with you? It is prolonged stress! The bottom line is that our thinking, manners, and choices have important implications for our well-being. The way we handle our thinking, manners, and choices determines our happiness as humans.

The Body

Flesh and bones define the mass of the body. In most cases, a person's closest inspiration comes from what they can feel and see with the sense. The body is not just the concrete structure that houses the man's vital organs and blood to operate; The body is beyond the framework we see outside. The body represents the energy that gives us breath, and the ability to utilise the breath for our life purpose is also stored in the body. This includes energy for our spirit beings and souls. The body is a very vulnerable part of our existence. It makes physical existence possible for us. In that way, the body is used to stir itself and gain access to our spirit and mind through meditation.

A study carried out in 2016 by the National Center for Complementary and Integrative Health (NCCIH) further supported the claim that meditation is a great method of repositioning and complementing the health of the body. The body can be used to heal itself through meditation. We also get to use it to heal our compromised spirits and damaged souls. People often try to do this through various meditation techniques. But the body also needs the spirit and the soul to keep being in the progressive state.

For instance, we get hurt sometimes with the body, which is revealed in the form of a scar. The body must get positive energy for the scar to heal, and the soul must be uplifting. What heals the scar are not just the drugs. The placebo effect has proven that to us. It is this energy that is released into the body and felt by the soul through the mind. The body serves as a repository of energy and a medium through which the soul can access the beyond for healing and salvation.

The Soul

A lot of people do get confused about the real representation of the soul. You sometimes ask yourself this, "Is it real?" "Is there a soul?" "Where is my soul if I indeed have one?" Various questions run through many people's minds, but the underlying essence of those questions is always the willingness of people to know and learn more about the concept of the soul.

Simply put, the soul is the spiritual and emotional aspect of you. It is that with which you feel a connection to the non-physical. This part of you is not detachable from the body. You cannot single it out for analysis or observation. The only time it becomes separate from the body is when the body dies. It is believed to exit the physical world as the body that houses it is already lifeless. The soul does many things to make up as part of your existence as a human being.

When the body ends, the soul does not end. It carries on the YOU. That is why the soul has been adjudged as eternal by many of the world's religions, including most Christian denominations, Hinduism, Islamic sects, and Buddhism.

Religion itself is a function of the soul. The soul connects to religious orientation so that the rites and faith performed seem acceptable to the soul. Hundreds of years ago in the Indian subcontinent, a wise scholar and Spiritual Master called Guru Sootaji believed that people become less and less aware of their spirituality or soul's existence as they place more and more emphasis on material things. To put it in a simpler form, there is an inverse relationship between prioritising worldly materials and growing in your knowledge and active involvement in the spiritual affairs of the soul.

Given that the soul lives forever, but the body is defected by mortality, it is more sensible to pay more attention to that which will last for a very long, perhaps endless, period. But in a surprisingly irrational twist, people seem to cherish the body and things in the world, forgetting that death is the fate of all living persons, in whatever ways it may come.

Interestingly, the soul determines the beauty of one's life. To make the most of life, you need to learn the importance of the soul and the techniques of engaging it always to place yourself on the right path. Although, some believe that the soul migrates from one life form to another. This implies that upon death, a soul leaves the lifeless body and takes on another. This is the philosophical basis of reincarnation in many quarters. However, one thing is uniformly acknowledged across the board – the soul's immortality is a fact upheld by Spiritualists, meditation practitioners, mediums and healers.

The Mind

In many cases, the mind refers to the thought faculty of the human being. A manifestation of your intelligence and mental infrastructure. That part of us that does the reasoning and consciousness. Yes, the brain is responsible for your consciousness as a human. The roles of the mind are dissecting issues, making decisions, and building knowledge and awareness. We can rightly say that the mind is the foundation of our rationality.

Once the mind is not working well or optimally, this becomes manifested in the affected person's behaviors. He is either defined as a person of a small mind or insane. The well functioning of the mind is, therefore, the gap between lunacy and sanity.

The mind is further divided into four components that help it work well. These are the thought, the imagination, the memory, and the human consciousness. The thought aspect of the mind helps you have ideas, think of solutions to problems, and know-how to face issues that come your way. Imagination is the creative engine of the mind; it makes analogies and concludes them. Memory refers to your ability to receive, process, store, retain, and retrieve information from the brain.

What could we probably do without memory? Getting ill with amnesia, forgetfulness, and learning difficulties indicates that the mind is not focused and needs to be corrected. Abstinence of the mind is beyond being unconscious for a few seconds but rather implies the mind is lost for long and can't comprehend the happening in the environment. If the mind remains absent for long, then it can't find a solution to the things happening in the environment.

How these three combine to define YOU in the world

Your body, soul, and mind are the fundamental components of YOU. They are the principal considerations in defining your personality as a whole. In most cases, they also decide your placement and treatment by society. Take the body as an instance. Society has such terms as healthy, unhealthy, beautiful, ugly, strong, weak, short, tall, able, disabled, attractive, unattractive, rich, poor, average, wounded, unwounded, etc.

These are some of the terms that people often use to describe and qualify the body condition. The soul is the spirit and emotional part of your being. People look at you and use one or more of such terms as kind, unkind, loving, unloving, helpful, unhelpful, courageous, fearful, resilient, impatient, happy, unhappy, faithful, unfaithful, sociable, unsociable, and others. All these are functions characteristic of the soul.

However, the mind also has its own. We have various tags that influence our perception of other people's minds. Some are seen as intelligent and unintelligent, smart and docile, creative and non-creative, high thinking and low thinking, brilliant and non-brilliant, etc. There are already laid down standards that we use to assess and place people under categories.

Many have been written off in the past as unintelligent or not smart, yet they ended up recording massive achievements that put these stereotypes to shame. This is where it becomes understood that there are just two views about you. The views are what people call you and what you call yourself.

There is, therefore, a difference between how one is perceived and how the person perceives himself. The self is an entity on its own, and it has to be seen as such. Another dimension is awareness of the self. The body, soul, and mind play a huge role in how society defines the self. This does not necessarily have to be the same with your very awareness of yourself. Self-awareness is me telling myself that "I am strong" when people call me weak. It is me certifying that "I am pretty when the societal standards say my facial expression is not appealing enough. Now you know it's either you choose to live in a world built by society, or you choose a world of freedom built by the power of your mind, soul, and mind.

The way you see yourself is against the things that they say about you. Seeing yourself is being aware of yourself in your way and on your terms. This is seen through the consensus of society about you. Self-awareness is built by looking inward at oneself. No, it is not being influenced by what others are saying. Close your ears to the noises coming from the outside.

Chapter Two

Why you should be self-aware

Look into the mirror. What do you see? Do you see a loser or a winner? Do you see yourself as a truly disabled person or as a person who can play in unique and different ways from the common views of people? You may be sick, and everyone knows about it. But not everyone thinks you have the capacity for recovery. Many may not be expecting you to bounce back as a whole.

A research was conducted in the U.S during the height of social segregation between the Whites and Colored People in America. In that research, some black kids were randomly selected to participate in a survey. They were shown two dolls – one white and the other black – and asked to say which of the two dolls was beautiful and ugly. They were also asked the reason for their choice. The result was shocking. All the black kids believed that the white doll was beautiful and the black one was ugly. When they were asked why the white doll was chosen as beautiful, they responded similarly – "Because it is white." When they were asked why the black doll was ugly, they replied, "...because it is black." Their consciousness of self-worth was virtually nonexistent due to the prevalent racism and eurocentrism at that time. Regrettably, many kids who grew up in that toxic environment gradually became self-aware as inferior to the white race.

This is what happens to people who rely on others to know and understand themselves. The consequences of that lack of self-awareness are always catastrophic for the individual.

Knowing yourself makes self-healing work.

Knowing you will help overcome a lot of problems that you face in your daily experiences. The basic is the ability the challenge you face when you are trying to accept who you are. Knowing yourself helps boost your confidence immensely, investing in you, the willingness, capacity, and level of information needed to accept yourself for who you truly are, not what others say you are.

This foundation is the true basis of self-growth and positive development. Let's look at the situation of Mr. Robbins. He struggled at work and always wondered why he was getting criticised by his immediate superior for submitting work reports below official standards. At first, he thought his immediate boss for criticism was maliciously handpicking him. He knew he did have difficulties with reporting quality when creating the timely reports, but he didn't think the results were as bad as his superior made it seem. He was seriously hurting and also burning inside. However, as time passed, he decided to look inward and study himself to know him and what was wrong. When he objectively compared his work reporting quality to the ones the Management accepted from other officers, he figured out that his work was really below the company's standard. He also understood that he had no problem with content but organising and arranging the content irresistibly.

Pinpointing this capacity deficit, he took an online course on content design and organisation to upgrade his performance at work. This is what knowing yourself does to you. It makes you accept your shortcomings and become the reformed best that you can be. It is like the case of Rohan, who suffers from grief. He is sad and devastated by the emotional hurts that he suffers. He often wonders why he can't stop crying every time. He is hardly moved by anything any longer. Then he discovers why he can't seem to get back on his feet after his loss.

He did a self-assessment and discovered that loving memories easily moved him. He does not just fancy the happy moments he had with people; he caresses and cherishes those experiences. This makes him more vulnerable to the despair that does come from grief. Due to this discovery about himself, he has to detach himself from the memories of his loss to heal faster. Changing his environment and other non-essential things that may remind him of this lost happiness will do a world of good in this case of his healing from depression.

You need to understand the margin between understanding what the world thinks about you and what you want in life. It is not as if what you think about yourself is always the real truth, compared to what is going on people's minds about you. For instance, people who nag a lot do not always accept that they are nags. And there is also a possible situation of people misbranding a concerned person as a nagging one.

Here, Jenny always had problems with her boyfriend because she believed he hardly made time for their love. The boyfriend, Smith, on the other hand, believed he was doing his best. He claimed that Jenny was an inconsiderate nag demanding a level of commitment she never herself gave to the relationship. Jenny was enraged when she learned about his opinion. But at a point in time, when she looked inward for an honest and reflective assessment of herself, she realised that she was the one that placed expectations that were overboard. She started to see areas where Smith's commitments had gone unreciprocated by her. She also noticed that Smith's show of love had been declining steadily, perhaps due to the constant fights and hurt they gave to each other. This honest and open self-appraisal made her see things from the perspectives of hers and others. They discussed these things and reconciled afterward.

Jenny overcomes her relationship by getting to know and accept herself better and taking relevant steps to modify the situation. In this way, knowing yourself helps decision-making. This can be applied in virtually all ways of life. Knowing ourselves makes us get much better at our jobs, marriages or relationships or friendships with others, and other aspects of life. Knowing oneself makes us better communicators and makes us more confident in ourselves. We can escape the disappointing trap of self-denial because we have self-accepted and are open-minded to constant introspective appraisal and repositioning. It follows that knowing yourself is fundamental to pulling yourself up from loss and hurts. And of course, this comes with lots of looking neutrally at you from within yourself, too.

Chapter Three

Understanding your SELF

How well do you know yourself? Well, you can't know yourself without understanding yourself. As basic as it sounds, many people do find it difficult to understand themselves. They can't just seem to know what they want. At every point, there is a new development that is detached from the status quo.

Understanding oneself is a continuous development task that takes a lot of commitment on the part of the individual. It's not just a one-off situation of waking up to self-realisation. More than that, there are steps to fully understanding yourself as a distinct individual and not an extension, imposition, or imitation. One big advantage you get in return from this process is knowing your true self, not the presumed or alleged one.

How this greatly helps on the path to self-healing has already been discussed in the previous chapter. Understanding usually comes after a systematic and dedicated process of aligning with reality. And the reality here is your true, plain self. Let's talk about the steps one after the other.

Using the Mindfulness Methods: Theta and Angel Energy Healing Meditation Techniques

The Thetahealing meditation and Angel Energy Healing techniques are mindfulness meditations methods. They seek to create a harmony of your spirit, physique, and psyche using the Theta brain. This experience ushers you into a pure state of mind, and you become connected to the divine, the Creator of all that is. This connection with the

Supreme Being that the Thetahealing and Angelic Healing techniques seek to achieve through focused prayer to the divine source energy who we acknowledge as the Creator of All that is.

Through the Creator of All, you can come to the true realisation you have always sought. Your connection creates a path to your enlightenment. But, it does not just stop at that; you open the doors to healing your physical, emotional, and psychological wounds through these unions. This is the extra benefit that comes with the knowledge purpose of connecting to the Creator of All.

You find out about the Creator, discover your undiluted self, and personify the principles of the ThetaHealing techniques. This always brings magnetic results based on certain conditions, however. Harnessing the benefits of Theta and Angel Healing for knowledge and self-healing requires certain levels of progressive commitment and purity of the heart. The meditations are designed to teach you how to discover, amass and deploy your psychic abilities via spiritual awareness. The meditation exercises can help achieve such cardinal points as follows:

Finding your life purpose

You can find your life purpose by reading and healing through Angels Energy Healing or ThetaHealing meditation classes. Understanding yourself helps you realise the huge potentials embedded in you. You start a new world of self-discovery, chattering new waters and foraying into your untapped territories of value. What is life without purpose, by the way?

Society does not have the perfect configuration setting in unveiling what one is made of. Many people have dreams buried in chasing after what society identifies for them as their supposed dreams. In the end, they end up getting frustrated and provoked. Some do know in their minds that they have some innate prospects to pursue some goals. Others do not even get to discover those dreams before they die. One of the essences of the ThetaHealing and Angel energy healing technique is to connect you to those thoughts and knowledge you have left unexplored in your subconscious, stirring up a will to make the destined relevance of your existence.

Uplifting your career and finances

Your career and finances get a boost when you start engaging in the ThetaHealing technique or Angelic connection because you start retracing your steps. Retracing your steps means doing away with activities that are not profitable to your body and do not give fulfillment to your soul.

Careers and finances usually fall under such a list. Many are not doing what they are called to do, so apparently, millions of people are in the wrong boat of professions. Taking ThetaHealing and Angel Healing therapeutic classes enables a switch from frustrating careers to more happiness-based and self-fulfilling choices.

The same happens in finances when you strike out unreasonable expenditures that are causing unnecessary and avoidable bottlenecks in your financial health. Your personal growth is threatened if you allow and nurture such financial hiccups in your life. In these ways, ThetaHealing and Angel Energy Healing allow you a breath of fresh life in these two dimensions.

Tackling Weight loss and other Health Issues

One of the ultimate core milestones of the ThetaHealing and Angel healing technique is the person being relieved from existing health problems. There are tens of hundreds to thousands of testimonies of wonders that have been performed through these meditations.

In addition, there are cases of people who suffered from certain health conditions getting cured of their sicknesses from within after they tapped into the healing and recuperative potentials of the Healing techniques of Theta and Angels Energies.

The method harmonises the seven chakras (energy centres) in thetahealing and 12 Chakras (energy centres) in Angelic healing in your body. It mobilises them in a spiritual connection with the Creator of All to provide life-changing results.

Weight issues are one of the common battles that people fight in their day-to-day health experiences. The transformation that comes with it is not exactly magical in any way. Of course, far from that, it is a product of either psychological or physical degeneration or both. And, the solution to that is what ThetaHealing is best positioned to achieve.

Fighting Depression and Anxiety

When people in all highs and accomplished in their fields of endeavor say they are battling depression, many always wonder what could be the reason for such. This owns to the fact that they belong to the elite category with access to the luxuries of life. Yet there is always news of people – rich and poor, healthy and sick, and others – committing suicides day by day.

The point is that depression can happen to anyone and it is not necessarily based on the person's social class. Just the same way, anxiety occurs right across every stratum of human existence. Anyone could have anxiety attacks.

A depressed person may feel hopeless, down, and has trouble with his appetite and concentration activity. Some Thetahealing experts believe that depression and anxiety, as respective products of unhappiness and fear, are created in our subconscious minds as patterns of beliefs and programs.

Thetahealing technique and Angels Energy Healing declutter that mind and make you discover by yourself how to start having transformative thoughts that repress those negatives on your mind and complement your good health. There are powerful stories of people healing from depression, panic attacks, and even such challenging sickness as cancer through Thetahealing and Angel Energy Healing meditation and therapeutic techniques. It gives a life-changing experience to participants who opt for the treatment to tackle the problems of depression and anxiety.

In these cases, many of the patients had trusted the Thetahealing technique and Angelic Energy Healing as alternatives or complementary healing mechanisms alongside conventional healthcare. In other words, this is not a way of telling you to ditch orthodox medicine for what Thetahealing technique and Angel Energy Healing has to offer you.

Rather, it is saying that these exercises work wonders and even do so better when complemented with conventional treatment.

Releasing Trauma

The thetahealing technique teaches you to connect to the Creator of all, the energy of light and love through your body, mind, and soul. The Theta state is that of absolute peace of mind and disposal of negative energy. It is a relaxed condition in which the subconscious is released and cleared out for real truths to come out. And it is said that "When you know the truth, the truth shall set you free."

In that same way, you can be free from despair, traumatic experiences, and disorders that give you nightmares and make your life an inconvenience even for yourself. When you apply the combined techniques of Thetahealing and Angelic healing, if you choose to, it will produce relief from these troubling thoughts, trauma will slowly let out of your system.

The energy responsible for your misery is traced, and its source is traced. After this, these meditation techniques' goal would be redirected to invoke positive energies and clear out the compromising ones.

Spiritual upgrading

Speaking about his ThetaHealing experience, Brian recalled saying, "I was asked to sit on a chair. The practitioner first tuned herself and went into a meditative state and started by asking for my permission to let herself see what is going on energetically. I obliged. She then started discussing what I was looking to change in my life and proceeded to a series of questions and dialogue to get to the bottom of the issue.

She asked into my past; about things, I could have done differently. After those questions, she started accessing my subconscious mind, bringing out repressed memories and unprocessed feelings. She showed me how to use muscle testing to see if those beliefs are the ones that are creating blocks in my life. I felt free after the session.

If you are not familiar with muscle testing, also known as Applied Kinesiology, it is a way to test your subconscious. Thetahealing uses muscle testing to test for belief programs in a client, so the ego is not in the way. Muscle testing is only used to test your subconscious beliefs, and they are not facts.

For example, you might test yes for "I am fat and ugly" when you are perfectly healthy and attractive. The statement may currently be true for you, but it is not fact. Brian's experience sums up one of the focal points of Thetahealing as through connection to Creator, and you get to clear your negative karmic patterns and limiting beliefs that keep you stuck in life.

Thetahealing can be used to address any physical/health conditions, mindset, abundance blocks, and all kinds of relationship issues. As a client, you can opt for trained practitioners who are licensed to conduct Thetahealing sessions. A typical appointment includes an intuitive scan, belief work, and healing.

The practitioner will probably show you how to do muscle testing to see your beliefs that may trigger the area you are seeking to change. Nothing is changed without your permission. The Thetahealer is trained to know what questions to ask to get to the bottom of belief. Sometimes they won't need to ask many questions because they also receive insights from the Creator.

You will get to understand the different levels of belief systems and your karmic patterns, and through muscle testing, the beliefs that are not serving you can be cleared easily. The practitioner will ask your verbal permission for every belief change and for any healing that is done.

The expected result is for you to heal and connect to the energy of higher vibrational forces. A Thetahealing session is much more than therapy and meditation. It is also a mix of spiritually elevating encounters that will forever change your story for good.

Making out time for reflections

The ThetaHealing technique and Angels Classes are meditative, therapeutic and make one spiritually conscientious. The permission you give for the practitioner's foray into the deep of your mind and chakras is evidence of your independence and capability for good.

The questions are meant to make you think back slowly into the past and figure out what could have happened differently or not happened at all. It is more of rewinding all back and saying, "Oh! Come to think of it…." That way, you can find out what has been going wrong. Also, using the Theta brain wave in this yoga-level meditative exercise will help connect the energies into your mind, body, and soul to the divine source for healing. For example, you get to know why you feel sad and overwhelmed with depression.

Ask Yourself Personal Questions

Are you happy? I mean, truly happy? That is not meant to be answered abruptly. It calls for deep reflections. Check the situations that you are in. Would they be what you would have wished for had things been different? Do you like being with people, or do you like being alone? How would you describe your personality in simple words? Do you feel comfortable right now where you are? You need to look back and talk about your capabilities too. What would you describe as your strong and weak points? Do you think you are unique as an individual? Why would you think so? Are you the competitive type? What could be your competitive interests? Why do you feel you are a loser? Is it a way of taking responsibility for your past errors? Why do you feel guilty and bitter? Do you believe in yourself? These are questions you should be able to answer from the depths of your heart. ThetaHealing sessions enable you to provide sincere answers to these questions, and this will set you better on your journey to getting healing and wholeness.

Theta and Angel Healing Classes help you reform your lifestyle.

Certain lifestyles are unhealthy to your body, soul, and mind. Thetahealing and Angel healing classes help you find out the wrong ways you have been living. You learn to live healthier and better. These are those habits that must have been detrimental to your soul and living.

Aiming to please others is one issue. You will find yourself always living by the standards other sets for you even if they are not going by the same. You are meant to grow at your own pace, not live by external expectations. You are not just a tool for the satisfaction or amusement of another person; rather, you deserve happiness on your own. The independence of will to pursue that happiness dictates that you don't live to always please others, even at the cost of your happiness.

Thetahealing technique and Angel classes will also teach you to appreciate who you are as a person and be confident in yourself. Yes, "belief in personal adequacy" is the right description of this wonderful feature you can get through the Thetahealing and Angel Healing meditation and spirituality session. This will make you increase your interest in yourself and learn more about who you are.

Don't forget that increased self-awareness is very positive for genuine self-healing to occur in a person. Self-forgiveness is also another big deal that ThetaHealing avails us of. The importance of coming to peace with yourself in the process of self-healing cannot be overemphasised. Internal harmony is one of the first objectives that the Thetahealing session aims to achieve before going further into other considerations. There are things we may have done in the past that we are not so proud of. It happens that such memories have continued to hunt some people in a crushing consciousness of self-guilt.

Some people might have already gotten state penalties if theirs were deemed criminal by courts of competent jurisdiction. Others may not have gotten a guilt sentence from the court, but they carry this moral burden on their minds, and has greatly affected their physical, spiritual, and emotional well-being. Self-forgiveness helps you to put this burden down safely, and Thetahealing meditation and therapy help you with that and more.

Many in the past who failed to forgive themselves sought escape from the torture of self-guilt through suicide. The Thetahealing and Angel Healing classes will help you learn to get protected from having such improprieties in your thoughts. After letting go of this grudge on yourself will help you learn from your mistakes and stop having negative thoughts and feelings about yourself. With this kind of new orientation and attitudes that you can achieve through the Thetahealing and Angel classes, you become better positioned to strive for your calls and drive them to fruition. You will find a hobby and do what you love that keeps you relaxed and free of stress.

Chapter Four

Doing the Healing – Energy, Theta, and Angels

ThetaHealing, as a meditation exercise, is not particular about any religion. It acts as a generalist approach to pursuing human happiness in day-by-day affairs. It is a spiritual ritual and philosophy state that helps to solve physical and spiritual problems.

Psychological issues such as depression, anxiety, panic attacks, and so on are also captured in the solution package. Vianna Stibal, the inventor of the ThetaHealing technique, used the meditative and therapeutic solution to heal a tumor on her leg miraculously.

The goal of ThetaHealing is to get connected to the Creator of All through a yoga-level meditation. The flow of positive energy from the Creator will facilitate the healing of sicknesses and other variants of impairments.

A fundamental principle of ThetaHealing is that our beliefs and emotions have their say on the state of our health. We get to take charge of these dimensions of human existence to correct wrong growths and other unwanted developments in our life.

The transformative power of ThetaHealing helps promote harmony of the body, spirit, and mind in peace, love, and care. There is a strong emphasis on love and affection because it is believed in ThetaHealing that it helps clear one's path off negative energy so that connection with the Creator of All is made possible through the concept of the seven planes of existence. We will discuss that in detail later on.

The Seven Planes of Existence in Perspectives

The concept of seven planes of existence helps us understand the conceptual framework of the ThetaHealing exercise and how it is carried out along physical and spiritual dimensions. It sets out to boost us on various levels and give us raises above our struggles in these aspects.

You might be wondering, "Why should I learn or understand the concept of the seven planes of existence?" Well, it is the fundamental manual that shows and defines the art of ThetaHealing.

According to Vianna Stibal, the founder of ThetaHealing, these seven planes of existence are the physical and spiritual forces of the cosmos or reality that explain the various dimensions of our universe and beyond. These forces of reality are really wide for the human mind to understand, so they must be in abstract form.

This is the basis of the emphasis on the human brain, which must be on a Theta frequency for an impacting meditation. The human brain can operate on any of five frequencies. They are Gamma, Beta, Alpha, Theta, and Delta.

The Theta frequency works for meditative healing because it provides the perfect state of mind to connect to the Creator of All. The Theta state of mind avails us the opportunity to see these forces of cosmos in their exaltedness through the Creator. Specific energy is assigned to each of the seven planes, and this energy is best known as a vibration. Aside from the uniqueness of the energy of each plane, one basic difference that sets one plane different from another is the frequency of the vibration and the spiritual and physical experiences of the residents.

The higher the frequency of vibration, the faster the speed of the objects. That accounts for why the molecules in the solid objects of the first plane move very slowly. The ones in the second one move faster than those in the third, and so on until it gets to the highest and fastest one, the seventh plane. These vibrations are regarded in ThetaHealing as the essence of life in all its forms.

Why Do We Connect to these Planes of Existence?

The moment you can understand the forces of vibration of these planes, you can influence the energy inherent in these forces of cosmos to heal yourself of any sicknesses or diseases and bolster your spirituality or fellowship with the Creator of All. But you can only access these vibrational forces of the planes of existence through the energy of pure, serene, and calm thoughts. The brain does this when it operates in the Theta frequency, a deeply relaxed, focused, and inward-oriented state of mind. It is the very stage of consciousness just before the sleep mode.

The Modus Operandi of the Planes

The planes are sectioned into very narrow coverings that assume the forms of beliefs that metamorphose into the subconscious state of every person on Earth. The moment one ascends unto the seventh plane of existence, all the coverings are dropped. At that time, the person realizes that they are not distanced from the planes but linked to them.

The rules, laws, commitments, and conditions that operate in one plane are essentially different from those in another plane of existence. The natural makeup of these planes stipulates that the first six planes, i.e., planes 1, 2, 3, 4, 5, and 6, encompass illusions. But there are no illusions in the seventh plane, which is the ultimate of truth and divinity. If your mind holds no impure thought and is in an extremely relaxed and serene state, it cannot comprehend these planes of existence.

Suppose you do not comprehend these forces of vibrations that define the planes of existence. In that case, you won't be able to connect to the Creator of All That Is and be part of the divine experience of prayer, supplications, and self-gratifying meditation.

How we are connected to the Planes of Existence

Every human being is a detailed combination of the Planes of existence. The body, for instance, is made up of five compounds that are different from each other. We have the liquids, carbohydrates, proteins, Deoxyribonucleic Acid (DNA), and ATP (energy).

It should be understood that each of these components of the body mass reflects at least one or more of the Seven Planes of existence. The other two components of our existence, the mind and the soul need our body mass compounds to be functional. If any of these compounds is lacking or troubled in one way or another, it will affect the mind and soul.

It is believed that when a person lacks the seventh plane of existence, the ATP, in his composition, this will occasion an emptiness of spirit and undiluted and no-strings-attached love. This is not good as the person involved will have his heart filled with bitterness, inhumanity, and spiritual incapacity. The lack of the seventh plane of existence, the DNA in human analogy, will cause the person's non-existence of a spiritual structure.

Who are Angels?

Angels are not just regular beings. They embody energy in its purest and finest forms, and they are also divine beings who are intricately connected to The Creator. Angels are the pathways of prayers and the messengers of hope from The Creator to us.

Doing these functions shows a great deal of bright light to illuminate our paths to achieving personal prosperity and becoming the best of ourselves. We cannot communicate with Angels in regular ways because they are spirit beings. Being humans, we are a unity of the body, spirit, and soul. So we need to turn on our spiritual consciousness to gain access to the angelic realm.

What is this Angelic Realm?

The Angelic realm is a spiritual environment where we connect to Angels and their energy powers, healing, grace, and pure energy. The composition of angels, that is, what they are made of, allows them to deliver healing to us and guide us with their compassionate and white loves.

Thus, angels are divine protectors and links between the Creator and us. Suppose you want to know Angels and how to connect to them for a wonderful healing experience. In that case, you will need to undergo Angel healing classes to be taught comprehensively about Angels and how to contact them to benefit from their gracious light and healing.

Types of Angels

Angels are divided into Angels and Archangels. The classification is more about ranking. Archangels are more powerful and endowed with responsibilities. They are like the Lieutenants of thousands in an Army.

The Archangels report directly to The Creator. Examples of Archangels are Archangels Michael, Gabriel, Raphael, Uriel, and others. These are the most popular on the list.

Angel Healing Classes and Invocations

Angels Healing Class is any platform that educates you about everything you want to know about Angels and how you can connect their benevolent energies. In a session, on the other hand, a certified Angel Healing therapist uses her expertise to make you experience the Angel healing.

However, you must bear in mind that connecting to the Angels for healing does not mean that your wounds and hurts will magically disappear. Rather, it is the process that needs the connection between the body, mind, and soul. It starts right from you believing and being spiritually conscious that your encounters with the Angels produce healing. Things will fall in place after that, gradually.

Why you should take the Angels Healing Courses

The first lesson they will give you in this class is a general description of the course and a brief explanation of the meaning and therapeutic experience of the Angel healing. Yes, that's right. We call it Angel Healing Therapy because it is a therapeutic experience. After that, you will get to learn about the protective and guardianship roles that angels play – the reason being that they are our divine partners in getting healing and connecting to The Creator.

This will make you aware of how Angels help us immensely with their shielding powers. You will also get to gain knowledge of the seven Archangels who are a top priority to us. Lastly, taking Angel healing classes will help you grow spiritually and develop your psychic ability, which is reading minds. At the end of your comprehensive training in Angel Healing and therapeutic manuals, you will become able and qualified to care for Clients and give presentations by deploying those client techniques and social interactions skills that you have acquired so far in the course of the Angel healing training.

Why you must connect to Angels of Energy Healing

One of the reasons is that connecting to these Angels of energy healing opens you to a wide range of limitless opportunities. Angels are very powerful as spirit beings, and they have this iron-clad resilience. This means that they will stop at nothing to deliver healing to you through their light energy. You just have to be relaxed and in a receptive state of mind for this tranquil business to occur.

Another reason is that the angels of energy healing can deliver healing to you at any time. This is because they are made of light energy, which means they can be promptly deployed to what they do. This includes helping you release all those negative energies responsible for your emotional troubles and depression, and illness even when you are asleep.

Third, the guardianship roles of Angels have been mentioned. Since they can see right into the future. Making an Angel of energy healing is like having a cheat code that helps you predict what is to come and prepare for it adequately.

Also, the more you connect to the Angels, the more you become aware of the spirit realm and what it entails. Since we all transmute back to spirit when we die, it is a case of familiarising ourselves with the place of eternal rest.

The most important benefit that you will get from connecting to the Angels of energy healing is the privilege to be connected to the Divine Creator. This is the ultimate of it all and the climax of the spiritual experience.

Chapter Five

Getting Stronger

You will get better and stronger only if you believe. You have to trust in yourself to be able to get through your challenges. To drive the prayers of your heart to fruition, you have to prepare your mind to be receptive to new ideas, beliefs, and patterns of living that are meant to propel you to solutions. For instance, reason dictates that you complement your meditations and prayers with a lifestyle that does not aggravate your problems. Getting stronger, in this case, is rising above traditional instincts and beliefs to make vital changes to One's life.

Getting stronger is knowing and acting that meditation has set you free from past behaviors that serve as obstacles to your healing. Now, pessimism is no longer an acceptable reaction to challenges. Rather, your soul becomes re-energised, and you start seeing hope even in extreme situations.

You are made stronger in character and deed by Thetahealing. Love becomes your operating guiding principle in behaviors and conduct. Growing stronger further impacts your level of conviction in the Thetahealing and Angel Healing processes. At this point, you are aware that, after being educated as a ThetaHealing or Angel healing Practitioner, you do not necessarily receive your healing as a cure.

What you receive from the Creator is what the Creator wants to give, not necessarily what you want. Under the presumption that the Creator knows and does best, we take every healing, maybe a cure or not, as the best thing we could receive at that point.

The Theta state of mind further strengthens and purifies your mind. The Theta frequency is the moment just before sleep, in a deep state of relaxed atmosphere and serenity. Scientists have upheld the claim that being in the Theta state of mind makes you stronger and better as a person. This is due to the tranquility you enjoy once you are in that state of mind. In that way,

ThetaHealing and Angels Healing make you stronger psychologically, spiritually, and physically. Also, the Thetahealing helps you achieve high verbal Intelligence Quotient I.Q. and develop verbal proficiencies, too. The ThetaHealing meditation trains you with the power of words and emotions, and spirits. The result of such sophistry that you get to accomplish through the sessions is having your way more with words as you employ greater verbal, spiritual, and psychological resources to navigate life's hurdles.

Your stress and worries get reduced through Thetahealing, so the health and well-being of your body, mind, and spirit remain a priority in the exercise. With this, you have what it takes to bring down such problems as depression and anxiety attacks that may be confronting you or trying to penetrate your well-being.

Lastly, Thetahealing and Angel Energy Healing Classes synchronise the two hemispheres of your brain. This aids your ability to summon clear, reflexive, mental picturing, and creativity in thinking. The result is to reduce pain, advance excitement, and upscale the release of endorphins culminating in increased happiness for you.

Chapter Six

My Story

The Formative Years

Growing up in Nepal as a child, life was more challenging as a mix of reality for me. It is not just about being emotionally conscious with hard-to-tame expressive tendencies in an average environment where life is stiff and centered on survival. The repression of One's inner cravings is defined as the conventional.

Indeed, I had to defy the odds to become the personality I am proud to project today. Don't get me wrong. As much as there are impediments to creating my reality as a speaker, a feeler, and a relatable, Nepal played a vital part in that journey of self-discovery and reality formation.

Through the Nepalese experience, I was able to know myself better. I figured out the challenges I face in life due to my personality and how to deal with all these. Of course, dealing with them was never easy. I find myself thinking a lot, even about the very few details that many other people may see as insignificant.

For me, every feeling, emotion, and drop of affection counts, and they easily influence my thinking, behaviors, and relations with people. However, I do not lack emotional or affective intelligence. Ultimately, I had to go on a mission to free my sanity, thoughts, and of course, my personality because things were simply not right.

Discovering my reality – my Buddhism experience in Nepal

For a very long time, I was in confinement. A little cell that restrained me from becoming and expressing the best and worst of me. I was simply discouraged from being me. "Oh, don't you cry!" "Big girls, don't cry" "Don't be weak!" Those were words spoken to me when I was young.

Consequently, I became self-repressive. I locked in energies that were meant to flow out. I couldn't realise my real self because I didn't explore the self. Not knowing my true self, I couldn't accept myself for who I am. This was the foundation of where it all went wrong. The basis was the psychosocial error that society pictures and practices as self-control.

The understanding that emotions are weaknesses that must be stampeded, not given attention. But what have we? A culture of self-denial and conforming to celebrated principles all for public perception?

In my case, I have always known something was wrong. Having to show brute even when the heart melts like butter is probably one of the moments I have faked. A relic of the cage made for me. In that cage, emotions, fears, love, affections, and other energies of self-expression are simply gaged. I asked questions for a long time. I had no peace within me, so, I was constantly running to free myself from these shackles.

In the course of my sojourn, I was met with a revelation, and I got delivered from hopelessly trying not to be me. What changed for me? My experience at the Shirdi Sai Baba Temple in India was the turning point for my liberation. I was able to find some degrees of internal peace through my experience in Buddhism while in Nepal.

Not that I was new to Buddhism. In my family, we have all had Buddha commitments in varying forms since I was young. This experience was somewhat relieving in a way I had never felt before. Buddhism helped me secure inner peace from my troubles. Truly, some people believe that Buddhism is a science of the mind. Considering how systematic and experimental Buddhism meditations are, the conclusion is not far from the truth. Meditation can be completed in such ways as deep breathing, chanting, and Yoga.

So who is Shirdi Sai Baba?

The late Shirdi Sai Baba was an Indian Spiritual Master and a Colossus who lived through the mid-19th and early 20th centuries. He pioneered the meditative dimensions of spirituality without any emphatic religious attachment. Sai Baba realised that it was possible to connect to the energies of the Heavens without going through any particular religious worship. Our spirits could be pathways of connecting to the Divine Being.

According to records, Sai baba once said, "Look to me, and I shall look to you" The statement was a testament of the capability for spiritual exchange with The Creator that the latter himself has deposited into the trio of Man's body, spirit, and soul. When we look deeply inward, we get to see Him, talk to Him, and listen to Him.

How? By utilising the introspective tissues of our conscious and subconscious states to form artilleries of communication with the Master of All. This is meditation in its purest and finest form, and that was what Sai baba embodied and preached. The Shirdi Sai Baba Temple in India is a veneration of those sacred principles that his life stood for.

How Shirdi Sai Baba Meditative Solutions Impacted Me Positively

In the year 2006, I went through a major emotional hardship. I remembered visiting the Shirdi Saibaba Temple in India at this time. At the Shirdi Sai Baba Temple, I had the consciousness of being reconnected with my identity that was lost to keeping up with social norms and dictates over my life. As I strove to achieve the ultimate mental state of peace and happiness, it occurred to me that meditation is a very potent instrument for mind control.

If I must get this right, I must explore these fields of introspection, relaxation, and reflection in all available ways. So after I came back from there, I had a strong desire to begin to meditate and understand more about meditation.

My Experience at the Vipassana Meditation Center

Before the meditative experience at Vipassana, I had always been fascinated by theories that explain acts of meditation and spirituality. I remember reading many books authored by various persons on these topics. So when circumstances compelled me to tow these lines, I readily embraced my reality. Located in the valley of Kathmandu, Vipassana was a subtle checkmate on my struggles with self-realisation. Right there, I was ably stirred so well that my consciousness which was previously on the fringes of illusion and painful thinking, metamorphosed into an experience of realness and exacting of identity. Simply put, I saw things the way they are.

This instrumentality of making one realistic and free from controlling energies was an old Indian technique. Rediscovered by Gutama Buddha about 2500 years ago as principles of universal healing and remedial forms, this technique is always set out to achieve the concurring observation and confirmation of the SELF by exploring the interconnections between the mind-body and soul. Throughout my 10-day stay, I learned to watch my thoughts, feelings, judgments, and sensations until they began to define my reality clearly. At last, I was free from the illusion of emptiness and the negativity of personal limitations due to imposed society norms, traditions, and bonds.

Becoming an Angels Healing Teacher

I attended the Diana Cooper School of White Light, and became a qualified Angel Teacher. The coursework of my training at Diana's centers on making people know more about their energies of the angels, and how they can connect with Angel's power in understanding the spiritually consecrated mysteries of the universe.

I became a qualified Angel Teacher for one central reason – to free myself and others from negative energies with Angel's power. Having suffered from internal turmoil and the general recession of the persona, I have been able to inspire people and avail them of what they need to tow that spiritual path. With my competency built from the Angles training, I have uplifted spirit beings from the shackles of problems and compromises, furnishing people with the self-confidence, courage, and insights they need to connect with the spiritual energies of the angels and Archangels and then come to light.

I teach people how to overcome their fears and worries and achieve the inner peace they crave for. Angels Healing classes aim to help you achieve your personal development in the various areas you want and help you build your practice. Inspiration and wisdom are some of the tools you get equipped with, and this will advance you to frontiers of knowledge that will help you succeed in your spiritual adventures. Angel Classes will help put your body, mind, and spirit in preferable dimensions in even more relatable terms.

As a qualified Angel Teacher who conducts the Angel Healing classes, I have certified proficiencies in conducting spiritual meditations and reeling out Archangels invocations and helping people to meet their Guardian Angels. This has endowed me with the privilege of access to tap this magnificent Angelic energy for the benefits and personal development of myself and my students with whom I hold Angel Healing Classes.

My Encounter with Angels and Archangels Superb Energy

Archangel Michael is the grand Angel who personifies God's protection, strengths, truths, and power to the Creator of All. Given this conduit role that Archangel Michael plays, he can convey our prayers to the Creator of All. Therefore, invoking Archangel Michael is like summoning the direct messenger of God to deliver your requests and guide you from external negatives that may want to tamper with your energy.

I had this revelation in the middle of a session with a Client. I was connecting to this beautiful energy, and in my vision, I was told that this energy was Archangel Michael. I learned about Angels through ThetaHealing and some books, but I was not very aware of the angels and Archangels. So this instantly took me back to when I was 18. I saw a book just before I left Nepal to live in the U.K. The book was titled "Little Light on Ascension" by Dianna Cooper. Although I had never read the book at that time, I knew that I remembered that I gifted that book to myself. I had completely forgotten about it until I started having this energy from angels connecting to me.

So I took the Angels Teacher Training to set out and explore the universe and angels. Because I believe that nothing is by accident, and there is always a deeper meaning to things thrown at us through the universe and higher power. So I felt like, "Okay, this is the time for me to learn about angels."

Becoming a Qualified Theta Healing Instructor and Practitioner

Becoming a ThetaHealing Instructor was something more than a coincidence for me. It indeed feels like I was destined to be an apostle of this technique, using it to better the lives of people around the world and provide training to others interested in knowing the psychosocial and spiritual relevance of ThetaHealing to mental health.

After taking and excelling in extensive training courses at various levels, I became a Thetahealing Instructor certified to provide qualitative learning developments in the subject. So it went like this. I came across ThetaHealing, and it worked like magic for me because it resonated with my life. So many of my childhood traumas are healed, and the memories which were repressed become awake. After experiencing the therapeutic wholesomeness that Thetahealing provides in its meditation exercises, I committed to making more and more people aware of and proficient in this practice.

In addition to being certified, I have travelled to many parts of the world to keep upgrading my skills. I have also studied counseling psychology and ancient knowledge, intending to integrate all of these to give clients a superb Thetahealing and meditation experience. I am passionate about helping individuals improve themselves spiritually and financially.

I am a mother of two and a fulfilled wife to a loving husband. I am not just a qualified ThetaHealing Instructor; I also have exemplary proficiencies in Angel Energy Healing as an Angels Teacher and a Reiki Master. I feel blessed to be endowed with so many skills and knowledge, and what gives the greatest joy is using all of these to educate people with the courses I provide and setting them right on the paths of rediscovering who they are.

Conclusion

We all experience different facets of life. All humans seemingly start in the same way, irrespective of the diverse material conditions. We all bleed the blood from our bodies. We all have souls that encode our spirituality. The mind, as a state of mental consciousness, began its evolution in every one of us. Yes, we all cry when it hurts, at least as innocent babies. As time goes on, the society that we live in begins to fill our minds with various orientations.

The deeper we get involved in these, the more drifted we become from the Creator's solutions as paths to true happiness. Our understanding of happiness gets distorted, and we are left with vanity at the end. Had we stuck to the true paths of the Almighty, we would have discovered how to be happy, healed, free, seeing, feeling, bonding, and being just the ideal human.

The way to achieve these is not just what we have been taught. Indeed, we need to explore appropriate energies in the physical, spiritual and mental realms to become the original version the Creator has of us. A version in which we are destined with the answers to all our questions. We only need to take our destinies.

So when we consider the gravity of problems that face us in our lives, we always need that assurance of a better tomorrow. A tomorrow of fulfilling a life purpose of love and a sense of universal duty to save the environment. This is us anticipating a triumph of affective emotions over inhumane repressions, hope over fear, and access to the Creator over being shut out in an impure state of unrefined energy.

Unfortunately, the long course of finding these answers reveals that the options are not many. A proven option is positioning the ThetaHealing meditation, Angel Healing Therapy, and practices of Spiritualism to combine all of these for our wholesomeness in the meditative consciousness of connection and fellowship with the Creator. With this, we can begin our walk into a future of what we deserve and becoming the Master of our own lives.

Printed in Great Britain
by Amazon

71096252R10024